Are We a Nation?

ADDRESS

OF

Hon. CHARLES SUMNER,

BEFORE THE

New York Young Men's Republican Union,

AT THE

COOPER INSTITUTE,

Tuesday Evening, Nov. 19, 1867.

PUBLISHED BY THE

NEW YORK YOUNG MEN'S REPUBLICAN UNION.

1867.

ADDRESS.

Mr. President :—At the close of a bloody Rebellion, instigated by hostility to the sacred principles of the Declaration of Independence, and inaugurated in the name of State Rights, it becomes us now to do what we can to provide that these sacred principles shall not again be called in question, and that the fatal pretension of State Rights shall not again disturb the national repose. One terrible war is more than enough; and since, after struggle, peril and sacrifice, where every household has been a sufferer, we are at last victorious, it is not too much to insist on all possible safeguards for the future. The whole case must be settled now. The constant Duel between the Nation and the States must cease. The National Unity must be assured,—in the only way which is practical and honest,—through the principles declared by our Fathers and inwoven into the national life.

In one word, the Declaration of Independence must be recognized as a fundamental law, and State Rights, in all their denationalizing pretensions, must be trampled out forever, to the end that we may be in reality as in name, a Nation.

Are We a Nation?

Are we a Nation? Such is the question which I now propose, believing as I do that the whole case is involved in the answer. Are we a Nation? Then must we have that essential, indestructible Unity which belongs to a Nation, with all those central pervasive powers which minister to the national life; then must we have that central, necessary authority, inherent in just government, to protect the citizen in all the rights of citizenship; and then must we have that other central inalienable prerogative of providing for the performance of all the promises solemnly made when we first claimed our place as a Nation.

"National" instead of "Federal."

Words are sometimes things, and I cannot doubt that our country would gain in strength and our people in comprehensive patriotism, if we discarded language which in itself implies certain weakness and possible disunion. Pardon me if I confess, that I have never reconciled myself to the use of the word "Federal" instead of "National." To my mind, our government is not Federal, but National; our Constitution is not Federal, but National; our courts under the Constitution are not Federal, but National; our army is not Federal, but National. There is one instance where this misnomer does not occur. The debt of our country is always *National*;—perhaps because this term promises in advance additional security to the anxious creditor. Liberty and Equality are as much as dollars and cents; they should be National also, and enjoy the same security.

During the imbecility of the Confederation, which was nothing but a league or *fœdus*, the government was naturally called Federal. This was its proper designation. Any other would have been out of place, although even then Washington liked to speak of the Nation. In summoning the Convention, which framed the National Constitution, the States all spoke of the existing government as "Federal." But after the adoption of that National Constitution which completed our organization as one people, the designation was inappropriate. It should have been changed. If not then, it must be now. New capacities require a new name. The word Saviour did not originally exist in the Latin language; but St. Augustine, who wrote in this language, boldly used it, saying that there was no occasion for it until after the Saviour was born. Even if among us in the earlier day there was no occasion for the word Nation, there is now. A Nation is born.

Meaning of "Nation."

There is something in the word Nation which is suggestive beyond anything supplied by the definitions of the dictionary. It awakens an echo second only to that of country. It is a word of unity and power. It brings to mind intelligent masses, enjoying the advantage of organization, for whom there is a Law of Nations,—as there is a Law of Nature,—each Nation being a unit. Sometimes uttered vaguely, it is simply an intensive, as in the familiar words, "only a *Nation* louder;" but even here the word furnishes a measure of vastness. In ordinary usage, it implies an aggregation of human beings, who have reached such an advanced stage of political development, that they are no longer a tribe of Nomads, like our Indians;—no longer a mere colony, city, principality or State; but they are one people, throbbing with a common life, occupying a common territory, rejoicing in a common history, sharing in common trials, and securing to each the protection of the common power. We have heard also, that a Nation is a people with the consciousness of Human Rights. Well did Louis the XVth of France exclaim, when this word began to resound in his ears: "What means it? I am king; is there any king but me?" The monarch did not know that the Nation was more than king, all of which his successor learned among the earliest lessons of the Revolution, as this word became the inspiration and voice of France.

The ancients had but one word for State and City; nor did they use the word Nation as it is latterly used. Derived from the Latin *nascor* and *natus*, signifying "to be born," and "being born," it was originally applied to a race or people of common descent and language, but seems to have had no reference to a common government. In the latter sense it is modern. Originally ethnological, it is now political. The French Communists have popularized the kindred word "solidarity," denoting a community of interests, which is an element of Nationality. There is the solidarity of Nations together, and also the solidarity of a people constituting one Nation, being those who, according to a familiar phrase, are "all in one bottom."

England early became a Nation, and this word seems to have assumed there a corresponding meaning. Sir Walter Raleigh, courtier of Queen Elizabeth and victim of James I., who was a master of our language, in speaking of the people of England, calls them "our Nation." John Milton was filled with the same sentiment, when, addressing England and Scotland, he says: "Go on, hand in hand, *O Nations*, never to be disunited; be the praise and heroic song of all posterity." In the time of Queen Anne, Sir William Temple furnished a precise definition, which foreshadows the definition of our day. According to this accomplished writer and diplomatist, a Nation was "a great number of families, derived from the same blood, born in the same country and *living under the same government*." Here is the modern element of living under the same government. Johnson, in his Dictionary, follows Temple substantially, calling it "a people distinguished from another people, generally by their language, origin *or government*." Our own Webster, the lexicographer, calls it, "the body of inhabitants of a country *united under the same government*." Worcester calls it, "a people born in the same country and *living under the same government*." The French Dictionary of the Academy calls it, "the totality of persons born or naturalized in a country and *living under the same government*." Of these definitions those of Webster and the French Academy are unquestionably the best; and of these two that of Webster is the most compact.

These definitions all end in the idea of unity under one government. They contemplate a political unity, rather than a unity of blood or language. There are undoubted nations where these do not exist. The various accents of speech and the various types of manhood, with the great distinction of color, which we encounter daily, show that there is no such unity here. But this is not required. If the inhabitants are of one blood and one language, the unity is more complete; but the essential condition is one sovereignty, involving, of course, one citizenship. It is in this sense that Gibbon employs the word, when, describing the people of Italy, all of whom were recognized as Roman citizens, he says: "From the foot of the Alps to the extremity of Calabria all the natives of Italy were born citizens of Rome. Their partial distinctions were obliterated and they insensibly *coalesced into one great Nation*, united by language, manners and *civil institutions*, and equal to the weight of a powerful empire." (*Gibbon: Decline and Fall;* Vol. I., p. 32, cap. II.) Here a dominion proceeding originally from conquest is consecrated by the concession of citizenship, and the great historian hails the coalesced people as a Nation.

One of our ablest writers of history and constitutional law, Prof. Lieber, of Columbia College, New York, has discussed this question with learning and power. According to this eminent authority, Nation is something more than a word. It denotes that polity, which is the normal type of government, at the present advanced stage of civilization, and to which all people tend just in proportion to their enlightenment and enfranchisement. The professor does not hesitate to say that such a polity is naturally dedicated to the maintenance of all the rights of the citizen as its practical end and object. It is easy to see that the Nation, as thus defined, must possess the elements of perpetuity. It is not a quicksand, or mere agglomeration of particles, liable to disappear, but a solid, infrangible crystallization against which the winds and the rains beat in vain.

State Rights.

Opposed to this prevailing tendency is the earlier propensity to local sovereignty, which is so gratifying to petty pride and ambition. This propensity, assuming various forms, in different ages and countries, according to the degree of development, has always been a species of egotism. When the barbarous islanders of the Pacific imagined themselves the whole world, they furnished an illustration of this egotism in its primitive form. Its latest manifestation has been in State Rights. But here a distinction must be observed. For the purposes of local self-government and to secure its educational and political blessings, the States are of unquestioned value. This is their true function, to be praised and vindicated always. But *local sovereignty*, whether in the name of State or prince, is out of place and incongruous under a government truly National. It is entirely inconsistent with the idea of a Nation. Perhaps, its essential absurdity in such a government was never better illustrated than by the homely apologue of the ancient Roman, which so wrought upon the secessionists of his day, that they at once returned to their allegiance. According to this successful orator, the different members of the human body once murmured against the "belly," which was pictured very much as our National Government has been, and they severally refused all further co-operation. The hands would not carry food to the mouth; nor would the mouth receive it if carried; nor would the teeth perform their office. The rebellion began; but each member soon found that its own welfare was bound up inseparably with the rest, and especially that in weakening the "belly," it weakened every part. Such is the discord of State Rights. How unlike that Unity, of which the human form with heaven-directed countenance is the perfect type, where every part has its function, and all are in obedience to that divine mandate which created man in the image of God. And such is the Nation.

Would you know the incalculable mischief of State Rights? Our continent furnishes three different examples, each worthy of extended contemplation. There are first, our Indians, the Aborigines of the soil, split into tribes, possessing a barbarous independence, but through this perverse influence kept in constant strife, with small chance of improvement. Each chief is a representative of State Rights. Turning their backs upon Union, they turn their backs upon civilization itself. There is next our neighbor republic Mexico, where nature is bountiful in vain, and climate lends an unavailing charm, while twenty-three States, unwilling to recognize the National power, set up their disorganizing pretensions and chaos becomes chronic. The story is full of darkness and tragedy. The other instance is our own, where sacrifices of all kinds, public and private, rise up in blood before us. Civil war, wasted treasure, wounds and death are the witnesses. All these with wailing voice cry out against that deadly enemy lurking in State Rights. But this wail may be heard from the beginning of history, saddening its pages from generation to generation.

Warnings of History against State Rights.

In ancient times, the City-State was the highest type, as in Greece, where every city was a state, proud of its miniature sovereignty. The natural consequences ensued. Alliances, leagues, and confederations were ineffectual against State Rights. The parts failed to recognize the whole and its natural supremacy. Amidst all the triumphs of genius and the splendors of art, there was no National life, and Greece died. From her venerable sepulchre, with its ever-burning funeral lamps, where was buried so much of mortal beauty, there is a constant voice of warning, which sounds across continent and ocean, echoing, "Beware."

Rome also was a City-State. If it assumed at any time the national form, it was only because the conquering Republic took to itself all other communities and melted them in its fiery crucible. But this dominion was of force, ending in Universal

Empire, where the consent of the governed was of little account. How incalculably different from a well-ordered Nation, where all is natural, and the people are knit together in self-imposed bonds. Then came the colossal power of Charlemagne, under whom peoples and provinces were accumulated into one incongruous mass. Here again was Universal Empire, but there was no Nation.

Legend and song have depicted the paladins that surrounded Charlemagne, fighting his battles and constituting his court. They were the beginning of that feudal system, which was the next form that Europe assumed. The whole country was parcelled among chieftains under the various names of duke, count and baron, each of whom held a district, great or small, where he asserted a local sovereignty, and revelled in State Rights; and yet they all professed a common allegiance. Guizot was the first to remark that feudalism, taken as a whole, was a confederation, which he boldly likens to what he calls the federal system of the United States. It is true that feudalism was essentially federal, where each principality exercised a disturbing influence, and unity was impossible; but I utterly deny that our country can fall into any such category, unless it succumbs at last to the dogma of State Rights, which was the essential element of the feudal confederation.

Feudalism was not a government, it was only a system. During its prevalence the Nation was unknown. Wherever its influence subsided the Nation began to appear. And now, wherever its influence still lingers on earth, there the yearnings for National life, which are instinctive in the popular heart, are for the time suppressed.

Curiously enough, Sweden and Hungary were not brought within the sphere of feudalism, and these two outlying lands, left free to natural impulses, revealed themselves at an early day as nations. When the European Continent was weakened by anarchy, they were already strong in national life, with an influence beyond their population or means. It was because they were nations.

Feudalism has left its traces in England; but it was never sufficiently strong in that sea-girt land to resist the natural tendencies to unity, partly from its insular position, and partly from the character of its people. At an early day the seven-headed Heptarchy was changed into one kingdom; but a transformation not less important occurred when the feudal lords were absorbed into the government, of which they became a component part, and the people were represented in a central parliament, which legislated for the whole country with Magna Charta as the supreme law. Then was England a Nation; and just in proportion as the national life increased has her sway been felt in the world.

France was less prompt to undergo this change; for feudalism found here its favorite home. That compact country, so formed for unity, was the victim of State Rights. It was divided and subdivided. The North and South, speaking the same language, were separated by a difference of dialect. Then came the great provinces, Normandy, Brittany, Burgundy, Provence, Languedoc, and Gascony, with constant menaces of resistance and nullification, while smaller fiefs shared in the prevailing turbulence. A French barony was an "autonomic government," with a moated town, in contrast with an English barony, which was merged in the kingdom. Slowly these denationalizing pretensions were subdued; but at last the flag of the French monarchy—the most beautiful invention of heraldry—with lilies of gold on a field of azure, and angelic supporters, waved over a united people. From that time France has been a Nation, filled with a common life, burning with a common patriotism, and quickened by a common glory. To an Arab chieftain, who, in barbaric simplicity, asked the number of tribes there, a Frenchman promptly replied, "We are all one tribe."

Spain also triumphed over State Rights. The Moors were driven from Granada. Castile and Aragon were united under Ferdinand and Isabella. Feudalism was overcome. Strong in the national unity, her kings became lords of the earth. The name of Spain was exalted and her language was carried to the uttermost parts of the sea. For her Columbus sailed; for her Cortez and Pizarro conquered. But these adventurous spirits could have done little had they not been filled with the exuberance of her national life.

Italy has been less happy. The pretensions of feudalism here commingled with the pretensions of City-States. Petty princes and petty republics, restless with local sovereignty, constituted together a perpetual discord. That beauty, which one of her poets calls a "fatal gift," tempted the foreigner. Disunited Italy became an easy prey. Genius strove in the bitterness of despair, while this exquisite land, where history adds to the charms of nature and gilds anew the golden fields, sank at last to become, in the audacious phrase of Napoleon, simply a geographical name. A checker-board of separate States, it was little else. It had a place on the map, as in the memory; but it had lost its place in the present. It performed no national part. It did nothing for imitation or remembrance. Thus it continued, a fearful example to mankind. Meanwhile the sentiment of nationality began to stir. At last it broke forth like the pent-up lava from its own Vesuvius, and Garibaldi was its conductor. Separate States, renouncing local pretensions, became greater still as parts of the great whole, and Italy stood forth as a Nation, to testify against the intolerable jargon of State Rights. All hail to this heroic revival, where dissevered parts have been brought together, as were those of the ancient Deity, and shaped anew into a form of beauty and power.

But Germany is the most instructive example. Here have State Rights triumphed from generation to generation, perversely postponing that National Unity which is the longing of the German heart. Stretching from the Baltic to the Adriatic and the Alps, penetrated by great rivers, possessing a harmonious expanse of territory, speaking one language, filled with the same intellectual life, and enjoying a common name, which has been historic from the days of Tacitus, Germany, like France, seems formed for unity. Martin Luther addressed one of his grand letters *An die Deutsche Nation*, To the German Nation; and these words are always touching to Germans as the image of what they desire so much. But thus far this great longing has failed. Even the empire, where all were gathered under one imperial head, was only a variegated patchwork of States. Feudalism in its most extravagant pretensions still prevails. Confederation takes the place of Nationality; and this vast country, with all its elements of unity, is only a discordant conglomerate. The North and South are inharmonious, Prussia and Austria representing the two opposite sections. But other divisions have been more perplexing. Not to speak of circles or groups, each with a diet of its own, which once existed, I mention simply the later division into thirty-nine States, differing in government and in extent, being monarchies, principalities, dukedoms and free cities, all proportionately represented in a general council or diet, and proportionately bound to the common defence, but every one filled with the egotism of State Rights. So complete was this disjunction, and such were its intolerable pretensions, that internal commerce, which is the life-blood of the Nation, was strangled. Down to a recent day each diminutive State had its own custom-house, where the traveller was compelled to exhibit his passport and submit to local levies. This universal obstruction slowly yielded to a Zoll Verein or Customs Union, under which these barriers were obliterated and customs were collected on the external frontiers. Here was the first triumph of Unity. Meanwhile the perpetual strife between Prussia and Austria broke out in terrible battle. Prussia has succeeded in absorbing several of the smaller States. But the darling passion of the German heart is still unsatisfied. Not in fact, but in aspiration only is Germany One Nation. Patriot Poetry takes up the voice, and scorning the claims of individual states, principalities and cities, scorning also the larger claims of Prussia and Austria alike, exclaims in the spirit of a true Nationality,

> That is the German's father-land
> Where Germans all as brothers glow;
> That is the land;
> All Germany is thy father-land.

God grant that the day may soon dawn when all Germany shall be one.

National Unity in our Country.

Confessing the necessity of a true national life we have considered what is a Nation, and how the word itself implies indestructible unity under one government with common rights of citizenship; and then we have seen how this idea has grown with the growth of civilization, slowly conquering the adverse pretensions of State Rights, until at last even Italy became one Nation, while Germany was left still struggling for the same victory. And now I come again to the question with which I began.

Are we a Nation? Surely we are not a City-State, like Athens and early Rome in antiquity, or like Florence and Frankfort in modern times; nor, whatever may be the extent of our territory, are we an empire cemented by conquest, like that of later Rome, or like that of Charlemagne; nor are we a feudal confederation, with our territory parcelled among local pretenders; nor are we a confederation in any just sense. From the first settlement of the country down to the present time, whether in the long annals of the colonies, or since the colonies were changed into states, there has been but one authentic voice; now breaking forth in organized effort for union; now swelling in that majestic utterance of the people, the Declaration of Independence; now sounding in the scarcely less majestic utterance of the people, the opening words to the constitution of the United States, and then again leaping from the hearts of patriots. All these, at different times, and in various tones, testify that we are one people, under one sovereignty, vitalized and elevated by a dedication to Human Rights.

Of the present thirty-six States, only thirteen were originally colonies. All the rest have been founded on territory which was the common property of the people of the United States, and they have been received into the fellowship of government and citizenship at their own request. If on any ground one of the original thirteen might renounce its obligations to the Union, it would not follow that one of the new States, occupying the common territory could do likewise. It is little short of madness to attribute such a denationalizing prerogative to any State, whether new or old. For better or worse we are all bound together in one indissoluble bond. The National Union is a knot, which, in an evil hour, the sword may cut, but which no mortal power can unloose without the common consent.

Common Citizenship among the Colonies.

From the earliest landing, this knot has been tying tighter and tighter. There were two ways in which it promptly showed itself: first, in the common claim of the rights of British subjects, and secondly, in the common rights of citizenship co-extensive with the colonies, and the consequent rights of every colony in every other colony.

The colonies were settled separately, under different names, and each had its own local government. But no local government was allowed in any colony to restrict the rights, liberties and immunities of British subjects. This was often declared. Above all charters or local laws were the imprescriptible safeguards of Magna Charta, which were common to all the inhabitants. On one occasion, the legislature of Massachusetts reminded the king's governor of these safeguards in memorable words, saying: "We hope we may, without offence, put your excellency in mind of that most grievous sentence of excommunication, solemnly denounced by the church in the name of the sacred Trinity, in the presence of King Henry the Third and the estates of the realm, *against all those who should make statutes, or observe them, being made contrary to the liberties of Magna Charta.*" (*Hutchinson's History of Massachusetts*, Vol. III., p. 472.) Massachusetts, on this occasion, spoke for all the colonies. Clearly the enjoyment of common rights was a common bond, constituting an element of nationality. In proportion as these rights grew more important, the common bond grew stronger.

The rights of citizenship in the colonies were derived from common relations to the mother country. No colonist could be made an alien in any other colony. As a British subject he had the freedom of every colony with the right of making his home there and of inheriting lands. Among all the colonies there was a common and interchangeable citizenship or *inter-citizenship.* The very rule of the Constitution then began, that "the citizens of each State shall be entitled to all the privileges and immunities of citizens in the several States." Here again was another element of nationality. If not at that time *fellow*-citizens, all were at least *fellow*-subjects. Fellowship had begun. Thus in the earliest days, even before Independence, were the colonists One People, with one sovereignty, afterwards renounced.

Longing for Union among the Colonies.

Efforts for a common government on this side of the ocean soon showed themselves. The Pilgrims landed at Plymouth in 1620. As early as 1642, only twenty-two years later, there was a confederation under the name of "the United Colonies of New England," formed primarily for the common defence; and here is the first stage of Nationality on this continent. In the preamble to the Articles the parties declare: "We, therefore, do conceive it our bounden duty without delay to enter into a present consociation amongst ourselves for mutual help and strength in all our future concernments, that, as in nation and religion, so in other respects, *we be and continue One.*" (*Palfrey's History of New England*, Vol. I., p. 624.) Better words could not mark the beginning of a Nation. A distinguished character of the time, after recording the difficulties encountered by the articles, says: "But being all desirous of union and studious of peace, they readily yielded to each other in such things as tended to common utility, so as, in some two or three meetings, *they lovingly accorded.*" (*Winthrop's Journal*, Vol. II., p. 99.) Encouraged by this "loving accord," another proposition was brought forward in Massachusetts "for all the English within the United Colonies to enter *into a civil agreement for the maintenance of religion and our civil liberties.*" (*Ibid*, p. 160.) More than a century elapsed before this aspiration was fulfilled; but here was the germ of future union.

Meanwhile the colonies grew in population and power. No longer merely scattered settlements, they began to act a part in history. Anxious especially against French domination, which already existed in Canada and was extending along the lakes to the Mississippi, they came together in Congress at Albany in 1754 to take measures for the common defence. Delegates from seven colonies were present, being from all north of the Potomac. Here the genius of Benjamin Franklin prevailed. A plan was presented by this master mind, providing for what was called "a general government," administered by a "President-General," where each colony should have representatives in proportion to its contributions, Massachusetts and Virginia having seven each, while New York had only four; and the first meeting of the "general government" was to be at Philadelphia. Local jealousy and pretension were too strong at the time for such a Union, and it found no greater favor in England, for there Union was "dreaded as the keystone of Independence." In defending this plan, Franklin, who had not then entered into the idea of Independence, did not hesitate to say, that he looked upon the colonies "as so many counties gained to Great Britain," thus using an illustration, which most forcibly suggested actual Unity. But though this experiment failed, it revealed the longing for one cis-Atlantic government, and showed how, under other auspices, it might be accomplished.

Scarcely ten years passed before this same yearning for a common life appeared again in the Colonial Congress at New York, convened in 1765, on the recommendation of Massachusetts, to arrest the tyranny of the Stamp Act, and assaults upon the common liberties. Nine Colonies were represented, and after deliberation they united in a Declaration of Rights common to all. Here was the inspiration of James Otis, the youthful orator of Freedom, whose tongue of flame had already flashed the cry, "Taxation without representation is tyranny," and that other cry, worthy of perpetual memory, "Equality and the Power of the Whole without distinction of color." Such were the voices that heralded our Nation.

An American Commonwealth.

The mother country persisted; and just in the same proportion the spirit of Union in the Colonies was aroused. Meanwhile that inflexible Republican, Samuel Adams, of Massachusetts, brooding on the perils to liberty, conceived the idea of what he called a "Congress of American States," out of whose deliberations should come what he boldly proclaimed "An American Commonwealth;" (*Wells's Life of Samuel Adams*, Vol. II., pp. 90, 94;) not several Commonwealths; not thirteen, but One. Here in one brilliant flash was revealed the image of National Unity, while the word "Commonwealth," denoted that common weal which all should share. The declared object of this burning patriot was "to answer the great purpose of preserving our liberties," meaning, of course, the liberties of all. Better words could not be chosen to describe a republican government. This was in 1773. As each Colony caught the echo it stirred with national life. Delegates were appointed, and in 1774 a Congress called "Continental," containing a representation from twelve Colonies, was organized at Philadelphia. The Congress undertook to speak in the name of "the good people" of the Colonies. Here was a national act. In the Declaration of Rights which it put forth, fit precursor of the Declaration of Independence, it grandly claims that, by the immutable laws of nature, the principles of the British constitution and the several charters, all the inhabitants are "entitled to life, liberty and property," and then announces "that the foundation of English liberty and of all free government is *a right in the people to participate in their legislative council*." (*Story's Commentaries on the Constitution*, Vol. I., § 194, *note*.) Here was a claim of popular rights as a first principle of government. Proceeding from a Congress of all, such a claim marks yet another stage of national life.

The next year witnessed a second Continental Congress, also at Philadelphia, which entered upon a mightier career. Proceeding at once to exercise national powers, this great Congress undertook to put the Colonies in a state of defence, authorized the raising of troops, framed rules for the government of the army, commenced the equipment of armed vessels, and commissioned George Washington as "general and commander-in-chief of the army of the United States and of all the forces raised or to be raised by them for the defence of American Liberty." Here were national acts, which history cannot forget, and their object was nothing less than American Liberty. It was American Liberty which Washington was commissioned to defend. Under these inspirations was our Nation born. The time had now come.

Declaration of Independence made a New Nation.

Independence was declared. Here was an act which, from beginning to end, in every particular and all its inspirations was National, stamping upon the whole people Unity in the support of Human Rights. It was done "in the name and by authority of the good people of these colonies," called at the beginning "one people;" and it was entitled "Declaration by the representatives of the United States of America in Congress assembled," without a word of separate sovereignty. As a National act it has two distinct features: first, as a severance of the relations between the "united colonies" and the mother country; and, secondly, as a declaration of self-evident truths on which this severance was justified, and the new Nation was founded. It is the "united colonies" that are declared to be free and independent States; and this act is justified by the sublime declaration, that all men are created equal, with certain inalienable rights, and that to secure these rights governments are instituted among men, deriving their just powers from the consent of the governed. Here was that "American Commonwealth," the image of National Unity, dedicated to Human Rights which had enchanted the vision of the early patriot, as he sought new safeguards for Liberty. Here was a new Nation, with new promises and covenants, such as had never been made before. The constituent authority from which it proceeded was "the people." The rights which it promised and covenanted were the equal rights of all; not the rights of Englishmen, but the rights of man. It is on this account that our Declaration has its great meaning in history; on this account our Nation became at once a source of light to the world. Well might the sun have stood still on that day to witness a kindred luminary as it ascended into the sky.

In this sudden transformation where was the sovereignty? It was declared that the *united* colonies are and *of right* ought to be free and independent States. It was never declared that the *separate* colonies were so *of right.* Plainly they never were so *in fact.* Therefore, there was no separate sovereignty either of right or in fact. The sovereignty anterior to Independence was in the mother country; afterwards it was in the people of the United States, who took the place of the mother country. As the original sovereignty was undivided, so also was that sovereignty of the people which became its substitute. If authority were needed for this irresistible conclusion, I might find it in the work of the great commentator on the Constitution, Mr. Justice Story, and in that powerful discourse of John Quincy Adams, entitled *The Jubilee of the Constitution*, in both of which the sovereignty is accorded to the people and not to the States. Nor should I forget that rarest political genius, Alexander Hamilton, who, regarding these things as a contemporary, declared most triumphantly that "the Union had complete sovereignty;" that "the Declaration of Independence was the fundamental Constitution of every State;" and finally, that "the Union and Independence of these States are blended and incorporated in the same act." (*Federalist, Historical Notice*, by J. C. Hamilton, p. 59.) Such was the great beginning of our national life.

Denationalizing Experiment of Confederation.

A beautiful meditative poet, whose words are often most instructive, confesses that we may reach heights which we cannot hold;

> "And the most difficult of tasks to keep
> Heights which the soul is competent to gain."

Our Nation found it so. Only a few days after the great Declaration in the name of "the people," Articles of Confederation were brought forward in the name of "the States." These were evidently drawn before the Declaration, and were in the handwriting of John Dickinson, then a delegate from Pennsylvania, whom the eldest Adams calls "the bell-wether of the aristocratic flock," and who was the orator against the Declaration. It was natural that an opponent of the Declaration should favor a system which forgot the constituent sovereignty of the people, and made haste to establish State Rights. These articles were not readily adopted. There was hesitation in Congress, and then hesitation among the States. At last, on the 1st of March, 1781, Maryland gave her tardy adhesion, and this shadow of a government began. It was a pitiful sight. The Declaration was sacrificed. Instead of "one people," we were nothing but "a league" of states; and our Nation, instead of drawing its quickening life from "the good people," drew it from a combination of "artificial bodies;" instead of recognizing the constituent sovereignty of the people, by whose voice Independence was declared, it recognized only the pretended sovereignty of States; and to complete the humiliating transformation, the National name was called "the style," being a term which denotes sometimes title and sometimes copartnership, instead of unchangeable unity. Such an apostacy could not succeed.

Even before this denationalizing framework was adopted its failure had begun. The Confederation became at once a byword and a sorrow. It was not fit for war or peace. It accomplished nothing national. It arrested all the national activities. Each State played the part of the feudal chieftain, absorbing power to itself and denying it to the Nation. Money could not be collected even for national purposes. Commerce could not be regulated. Justice could not be administered. Rights could not be secured. Congress was without coercive power and could act only through the local sovereignty. National Unity was impossible, and in its stead was a many-headed pretension. The country was lapsing into chaos.

Efforts for Nationality.

There were two voices which in this darkness made themselves heard, both speaking for National Unity on the foundation of Human Rights. The singular accord between the two, not only in sentiment, but also in language and in the date of utterance, attests a concert of action. One voice was that of Congress in an address on the close of the war, bearing date 18th April, 1783, where, after calling for larger powers in order to maintain the public credit, it was said in words worthy of companionship with the immortal Declaration: "Let it be remembered that it has ever been the pride and boast of America that *the rights for which she contended were the rights of human nature.*" (*Hickey's Constitution*, p. 140.) The other voice was that of Washington, in a general order, also bearing date 18th April, 1783, announcing the close of the war, where, after declaring his "rapture," in the prospects before the country, he says, "Happy, thrice happy shall they be pronounced hereafter who have contributed anything, who have performed the meanest office in erecting *this stupendous fabric of freedom and empire; who have assisted in protecting the rights of human nature.*" (*Sparks' Washington*, Vol. VIII., p. 568.) This appeal was followed by a circular letter to the governors, dated at Headquarters, where, after saying that it was for the United States to determine "whether they will be respectable and prosperous or contemptible and miserable *as a Nation*," Washington proceeds to name first among the things essential to National well-being, if not even to National existence, what he calls "an indissoluble union of the States under one head;" and he adds also that there must be a forgetfulness of "local prejudices and politics," and that "liberty" must be at the foundation of the whole structure. (*Ibid*, p. 443.) Soon afterwards appearing before Congress to surrender the trust committed to him as commander-in-chief, he hailed the United States as a "Nation," and also as "our dearest country," thus embracing the whole in his heart, as for seven years he had defended the whole by his prudence and valor. (*Ibid*, p. 504.)

An incident of a different character testified to the consciousness of National Unity. The vast outlying territory, unsettled at the beginning of the war, and wrested from the British crown by the common blood and treasure, was claimed as a common property, subject to the disposition of Congress for the general good. One by one, the States yielded their individual claims. The cession of Virginia comprehended all that grand region north-west of the Ohio, fertile and rich beyond imagination, where are now prosperous States rejoicing in the Union. All these cessions were on the condition that the lands "should be disposed of for the common benefit, and be settled and formed into distinct *republican States.*" Here was a National act with a promise of republican government, which was the forerunner of the guaranty of a republican government in the Constitution of the United States.

The best men, in their longing for National Unity, all concurred in the necessity of immediate action to save the country. Foremost in time, as in genius, was Alexander Hamilton, who was prompt to insist that Congress should have "complete sovereignty except as to that part of internal police which relates to the right of property and life among individuals and to raising money by internal taxes;" and still further, in words which harmonized with the Declaration of Independence, that "the fabric of the American empire should rest on the solid basis of the consent of the people." (*Historical Notice prefixed to J. C. Hamilton's edition of Federalist*, pp. 22, 59.) In kindred spirit, Schuyler announced "the necessity of a *supreme and coercive power* in the government of these States." (*Ibid*, p. 24.) Hamilton and Schuyler were both of New York, which, with such representatives, naturally took the lead in solemn resolutions, which, after declaring that "the situation of these States is in a peculiar manner critical," and that "the present system exposes the common cause to precarious issue," concluded with a call for a "general convention specially authorized to revise and amend the Confederation." Such was the movement which ended in the National Convention. Other States followed, and Congress recommended it as "the best means of obtaining a form of National Government." Meanwhile, Noah Webster, whom you know so well as the author of the popular dictionary, in an essay on the situation, published at the time, proposed "a new system of government, which should act, not on the States, but directly on individuals, and vest in Congress full power to carry its laws into effect." (*Eliot's Debates*, Vol. V., p. 118.) Thus simply was the case stated; but this proposition involved nothing less than a National government with supreme powers to which the States should be subordinate.

Jay, Madison and Washington anxious for Nationality.

Here I mention three illustrious characters, who at this time lent the weight of their great names to the national cause,—Jay, Madison and Washington,—each in his way without a peer. I content myself with a few words from each. John Jay, writing to John Adams, at the time our Minister in London, under date of 4th May, 1786, says: "One of the first wishes of my heart is to see the people of America become *One Nation in every respect;* for, as to separate legislatures, I would have them considered with relation to the confederacy *in the same light in which counties stand* to the States of which they are parts, viz., merely as districts to facilitate the purposes of domestic order and good government." (*Life of Jay*, Vol. I., 249.) Even in this strong view Jay was not alone. Franklin had already led in likening the colonies to "so many counties." Madison's desires were differently expressed. After declaring against "the individual independence of the States" on the one side, and "the consolidation of the States into one simple republic" on the other side, he sought what he called "a middle ground," which, if it varied from that of Jay, was essentially national. He would have "*a due supremacy of the National authority* and leave in force the local authorities so far as they can be subordinately useful." (*Eliot's Debates*, Vol. V., p. 107.) Here is the definition of a Nation. Washington stated the whole case with his accustomed authority in a letter to Jay, dated 1st August, 1786. After insisting upon the importance of a "coercive power," he then pleads for national life, saying: "I do not conceive we can exist long as *a Nation* without having lodged somewhere a power which will pervade the whole Union in *as energetic a manner as the authority of the State governments extends over the several States*." And he then adds: "To be fearful of investing Congress, constituted as that body is, with *ample authority for National purposes*, appears to me the very climax of popular absurdity and madness." (*Sparks' Washington*, Vol. IX., p. 187.) Such were the longings of patriots, all filled with a passion for country. But Washington went still further, when on another occasion he denounced State Sovereignty as "that bantling" and even "that monster." (*Jay's Life*, Vol. I. p. 258.)

The National Convention.

The Convention, often called Federal, better called National, assembled at Philadelphia in May, 1787. It was a memorable body, whose deliberations have made an epoch in the history of government. Jefferson and John Adams were at the time abroad in the foreign service of the country; Samuel Adams was in service at home in Massachusetts, and Jay in New York; but Washington, Franklin, Hamilton, Madison, Gouveneur Morris, George Mason, Wilson, Ellsworth and Sherman appeared among its members. Washington by their unanimous voice became President; and according to the rules of the Convention, on adjournment, every member stood in his place until the President had passed. Here is a glimpse of that august body which art may yet picture. Who would not be glad to look upon Franklin, Hamilton and Madison, standing in their places while Washington passed.

"*National*," not "*Federal*," in the Convention.

On the first day after the adoption of the rules, Edmund Randolph of Virginia opened the great business. He began by announcing among other things that a "Federal government" could not produce order or suppress rebellion; that a "Federal government" could not defend itself against encroachments from the States, and insisting that the remedy must be found in "the republican principle," concluded with a series of propositions contemplating a "National government," with what he called a "National" legislature in two branches, a "National" executive, and a "National" judiciary, the whole crowned by the guarantee of a republican government in each State. This series of propositions was followed the next day by a simple statement in the form of a resolution, where, after setting forth the insufficiency of "a union of the States merely Federal," or of "treaties among the States as individual sovereignties," it was declared "that a *National Government ought to be established*, consisting of a supreme legislative, executive and judiciary." Better words could not have been chosen to express the prevailing aspiration for national life. The resolution in this form was adopted after ample debate. At a later stage, in seeming deference to mistaken sensibilities, the word "National" was dropped, and the term "a government of the United States" was inserted in its stead; but the latter term equally denoted National Unity, although it did not use the word. The whole clause afterwards found a noble substitute in the Preamble to the Constitution, which is the annunciation of a National Government, proceeding directly from the people, like the Declaration of Independence itself.

From the beginning to the end of its debates, the Convention breathed the same patriotic fervor. Amidst all difference in details, and above the persistent and sinister contest for the equal representation of the States, great and small, the sentiment for Unity found constant utterance. I have already mentioned Madison, and Hamilton, who wished a National government; but there were others not less decided. Gouveneur Morris began early by explaining the difference between "Federal" and "National." The former implied "a mere compact, resting on the good faith of the parties;" the latter "had a complete and compulsive operation." (*Eliot's Debates*, Vol. V, p. 133.) Constantly this impassioned statesman protested against State Rights, insisting that the States were "nothing more than colonial corporations;" (*Ibid*, p. 286;) and exclaiming on one occasion, that "we cannot annihilate them, but we may take out the teeth of the serpents." (*Ibid*, p. 277.) Wilson was a different character, gentle by nature, but informed by studies in jurisprudence and by the education which he had brought from his Scottish home. He was for a National government, and did not think it inconsistent with "the lesser jurisdiction of States," which he would preserve; he would not "extinguish these planets, but keep them in their proper orbits for subordinate purposes." (*Ibid*, p. 169.) He was too much of a jurist to admit "that when the colonies became independent of Great Britain, they became independent of each other," and he insisted that they became independent, "not individually, but unitedly." (*Ibid*, p. 231.) Elbridge Gerry, of Massachusetts, was as strong on this point as Gouveneur Morris, insisting that "we never were independent States, were not so now, and never could be, even on the principles of the Confederation." (*Ibid*, p 259.) Rufus King, also of Massachusetts, touched a higher key when he wished that "every man in America should be secured in all his rights," and that these should not be "sacrificed by the phantom of State Sovereignty." (*Ibid*, p. 267.) Good words, worthy of him, who already in the Continental Congress had moved the prohibition of slavery in the National territories. And Charles Pinckney, of South Carolina, said in other words of far-reaching National significance that, "every freeman has a right to *the same protection and security*," and then again that, "Equality is the leading feature of the United States." (*Ibid*, pp. 233, 235.) Under such influences the Constitution was adopted by the Convention.

The National Constitution.

It is needless to dwell on its features, all so well-known; but there are certain points which must not be disregarded now. There is especially the beginning. Next after the opening words of the Declaration of Independence, the opening words of the Constitution are the grandest in history. They sound like a majestic overture, fit prelude to the transcendent harmonies of National life on a theatre of unexampled proportions. Though familiar, they cannot be too often repeated; for they are in themselves an assurance of popular rights and an epitome of National duties:—"*We, the people of the United States*, in order to form a more perfect union, establish justice, insure domestic tranquillity, provide for the common defence, promote the general welfare, and secure the blessings of liberty to ourselves and our posterity, do ordain and establish this Constitution for the United States of America." Thus, by the people of the United States was the Constitution ordained and established; not by the states, nor even by the people of the several states, but by the *people of the United States* in their aggregate individuality. Nor is it a league, alliance, agreement, compact, or confederation, but it is a constitution, which in itself denotes an indivisible unity under one supreme law, permanent in character; and this constitution, thus ordained and established, has for its declared purposes nothing less than liberty, justice, domestic tranquillity, the common defence, the general welfare, and a more perfect union, all of which are essentially National, and to be maintained by the National arm. The work thus begun was completed by three further provisions: first, that lofty requirement, that "the United States shall guaranty to every state in the Union a republican form of government," thus subjecting the states to the presiding judgment of the Nation, which is left to determine the definition of a republican government; secondly, the practical investiture of Congress with the authority "to make all laws necessary and proper for carrying into execution all the powers vested by this Constitution in the government of the United States, or in any department thereof," thus assuring the maintenance of the National government, and the execution of its powers through a faithful Congress chosen by the people; and thirdly, the imperial declaration, that "this Constitution, and the laws of the United States in pursuance thereof, and all treaties under the authority of the United States, shall be *the supreme law of the land, any thing in the Constitution or laws of any State to the contrary notwithstanding*," thus forever fixing the supremacy of the National government on a pinnacle above all local constitutions and laws. And thus did our country again assume the character and obligations of a Nation. Its first awakening was in the Declaration of Independence; its second was in the National Constitution.

Consolidation of our Union.

On its adoption the Constitution was transmitted to Congress with a letter from Washington, where, among other things, it is said that "in all our deliberations we kept steadily in view that which appears to us the greatest interest of every true American—*the Consolidation of our Union*—in which is involved our prosperity, safety, perhaps our national existence." (*Hickey's Constitution*, p. 188.) It is enough that this letter is signed George Washington; but it is not to be considered merely as the expression of his individual sentiments. It was unanimously adopted by the Convention, on the report of the committee that made the final draft of the Constitution itself, so that it must be considered as belonging to this great transaction. By its light the Constitution must be read. If any body is disposed to set up the denationalizing pretensions of State Rights under the Constitution, let him bear in mind this explicit declaration, that throughout all the deliberations of the Convention, the one object kept steadily in view was the *Consolidation of our Union.* Such is the unanimous testimony of the Convention, authenticated by George Washington.

The Constitution was next discussed in the States. It was vindicated as creating a National government, and it was opposed also on this very ground. Thus from opposite quarters comes concurring testimony. In Connecticut, Mr. Johnson, who had been chairman of the committee that reported the final draft, said in reply to the inquiries of his constituents, "that the Convention had gone upon entirely new ground; that they had formed *One new Nation* out of individual States." (*Webster's Works*, Vol. III, p. 479.) George Mason of Va., proclaimed at home that "the Confederation of States was entirely changed into *one consolidated government;*" and he repeated that it was "a *National* government, and no longer a Confederation." (*Eliot's Debates*, Vol. III., p. 29.) Patrick Henry, in his vigorous opposition to the adoption of the Constitution, testified to the completeness with which the work of consolidation had been accomplished. Inquiring by what authority the Convention had assumed to make such a government, he exclaimed: "That this is a consolidated government is demonstrably clear. * * Give me leave to demand what right had they to say, *We, the people?* Who authorized them to speak the language of *We, the people*, instead of *We, the States?* If the States are not the agents of the compact, it must be one great consolidated government of the people of all the States." (*Ibid*, p. 22.) Then again on another occasion the same fervid orator declared with infinite point: "The question turns, Sir, on that poor little thing, the expression, *We, the people*, instead of *the States*." (*Ibid*, p. 44.) Patrick Henry was right. The question did turn on that grand expression, *We the people*, in the very frontispiece of the Constitution, filling the whole with life-giving power, and so long as it stands there, the denationalizing pretensions of State Rights must shrink into nothingness. Originally "one people" during colonial days, we have been unalterably fixed in this condition by two National acts: first the Declaration of Independence, and then again the National Constitution. Thus has that original Unity in which we were born been doubly assured.

Other Tokens of Nationality.

There are other tokens of Nationality, which, like the air we breathe, are so common, that they hardly attract attention; but each has a character of its own. They belong to the "unities" of our Nation.

National Flag.

(1.) There is the National Flag. He must be cold indeed, who can look upon its folds rippling in the breeze without pride of country. If he be in a foreign land, the flag is companionship and country itself, with all its endearments. Who, as he sees it, can think of a State merely? Whose eyes, once fastened upon its radiant trophies, can fail to recognize the image of the whole Nation? It has been called "a floating piece of poetry;" and yet I know not if it have an intrinsic beauty beyond other ensigns. Its highest beauty is in what it symbolizes. It is because it represents all, that all gaze at it with delight and reverence. It is a piece of bunting lifted in the air; but it speaks sublimely, and every part has a voice. Its stripes of alternate red and white proclaim the original *union* of thirteen states to maintain the Declaration of Independence. Its stars of white on a field of blue proclaim that *union* of states constituting our National constellation, which receives a new star with every new state. The two together signify union, past and present. The very colors have a language, which was officially recognized by our fathers. White is for purity; red, for valor; blue, for justice. And all together, bunting, stripes, stars and colors, blazing in the sky, make the flag of our country, to be cherished by all our hearts, to be upheld by all our hands.

Not at once did this ensign come into being. Its first beginning was in the camp before Boston, and it was announced by Washington in these words: "The day which gave being to the new army, we hoisted the *Union flag*, in compliment to the United Colonies." (*Schuyler Hamilton on American Flag*, p. 55.) The National forces and the National Flag began together. Shortly afterwards, a fleet of five sail left Philadelphia amidst the acclamations of the people, according to the language of the time, "under the display of a *Union flag*, with thirteen stripes." (*Ibid*, p. 65.) This was probably the same flag, not yet matured into its present form. In its corner, where are now the stars, were the crosses of St. George and St. Andrew, red and white, originally representing England and Scotland, and when conjoined, after the union of those two countries, known as the *Union*. To these were added the thirteen stripes, alternate red and white, and the whole was hailed at the time as the *Great Union Flag*. The states represented by the stripes were here in subordination to the National Unity, represented by the two crosses. But this form did not continue long. Congress, by a resolution adopted 14th June, 1777, and made public 3d September, 1777, determined "that the Flag of the United States be thirteen stripes, alternate red and white; that *the Union* be thirteen stars, white on a blue field, representing a new constellation." Here the crosses of St. George and St. Andrew gave place to white stars on a blue field; the familiar symbol of British *Union* gave place to another symbol of *Union*, peculiar to ourselves; and this completed our National Flag, which a little later floated at the surrender of Burgoyne. Long afterward, in 1818, it was provided by Congress that a star be added on the admission of a new state, "to take effect on the fourth of July next succeeding such admission." Thus in every respect, and at each stage of its history, the National Flag testifies to the National Unity. The whole outstretched, indivisible country is seated in its folds.

There is a curious episode of the National Flag, which is not without its value. As far back as 1754, Franklin, while attempting to bring about a union of the colonies, pictured them in a wood cut under the device of an elongated snake cut into thirteen parts with the initials of a colony on each part, and under the disjointed whole the admonitory motto, "Join or die,"—thus indicating the paramount necessity of union. Afterwards in the heats of the revolutionary discussion, this representation was adopted as the head-piece of newspapers, and was painted on banners; but when the union was accomplished the divisions and initials were dropped and the snake was exhibited whole, coiled in conscious power, with thirteen rattles, and under it another admonitory motto, "Don't tread on me,"—being a warning to the mother country. This flag was yellow, and it became the early standard of the revolutionary navy, being hoisted for the first time by Paul Jones with his own hands. It had a further lesson. A half-formed additional rattle was said by Franklin to represent "the province of Canada," and the wise man added that "the rattles are united together so as never to be separated but by breaking to pieces." Thus the snake at one time pictured the necessity of union and at another time its indissoluble bond. But these symbols were all in harmony with the National Flag, which from its first appearance, in all its forms, pictured the common cause.

National Motto.

(2.) There is next the National Motto, as it appears on the national seal and on the national money. A common seal and common money are signs of National Unity. In each the supreme sovereignty of the Nation is manifest. The first is like the National Flag, and stands for the Nation, especially in treaties with foreign powers. The second is a national convenience, if not necessity, which takes its distinctive character from the Nation, so that everywhere it is a representative of the Nation. Each has the same familiar motto, *E pluribus Unum*, a Latin phrase, which signifies, *From many One*. Its history attests its significance.

On the 4th July, 1776, the very day of Independence, Benjamin Franklin, John Adams and Thomas Jefferson were appointed a committee to prepare a device for a Great Seal. They were the identical committee that had already reported the Declaration of Independence itself. Their report on the seal was made 10th August, 1776; and here we first meet the National Motto, which is in such entire harmony with the Declaration by which we were made "one people." Questions of detail intervened, and no conclusion was reached until 13th June, 1782, when the present seal was adopted, being the American bald eagle, with the olive branch in one talon and a bundle of thirteen arrows in the other, and in his beak a scroll, bearing the inscription, *E pluribus Unum*. Familiar as these words have become,—so that they haunt the memory of manhood, youth and childhood alike,—it is not always considered how completely and simply they tell the story of our national life. Out of many colonies was formed One Nation. Former differences were merged in this Unity. No longer many, they were one. The Nation by its chosen motto repeats perpetually, "We are one;" and the Constitution echoes back, "We, the people of the United States."

National Name.

(3.) There is next the National Name, which of itself implies National Unity. The States are not merely allied, associated, coalesced, confederated, but they are *united*, and the constitution, formed to secure a more perfect union, is "for the United States of America," which term was used as the common name of the Nation.

A regret has been sometimes expressed by patriots and by poets, that some single term was not originally adopted, which of itself should exclude every denationalizing pretension, and be a talisman for the heart to cherish and for the tongue to utter—as when Nelson gave his great watch-word at Trafalgar, "*England* expects every man to do his duty." Occasionally it has been proposed to call the country Columbia, and thus restore to the great discoverer at least a part of the honor which was taken from him when the continent was misnamed America. Alleghania has also been proposed, but this word is too obviously a mere invention, besides its unwelcome suggestion of alligator. Another proposition has been Vinland, being the name originally given by the Northmen, four centuries before Christopher Columbus. Professor Lieber, on one occasion, called the nation Freeland, a name to which it will be soon entitled. Even as a bond of union such a name would not be without value. As long ago as Herodotus, it was said of a certain people, that they would have been the most powerful in the world, if they had been united, but this was impossible from the want of a common name.

Forgetting that the actual name implies Unity, and when we consider its place in the preamble of the Constitution, that it implies Nationality also, the partisans of State Rights argue from it against even the idea of country; and here I have a curious and authentic illustration. In reply to an inquirer, who wished a single name, Mr. Calhoun exclaimed, "Not at all; we have no name because we ought to have none; we are only States united, and have no country." Alas! if it be so; if this well-loved land, for which so many have lived, for which so many have died, is not our country. But this strange utterance shows how completely the poison of these pretensions had destroyed the common sense as well as the patriotism of this much mistaken man.

Names may be given by sovereign power to new discoveries or settlements; but, as a general rule, they grow out of the soil. They are autochthonous. Even Augustus, when ruling the

Roman world, confessed that he could not make a new word, and Plato tells us that "a creator of names is the rarest of human creatures." Reflecting on these things we may appreciate something of the difficulty in the way of a new name at the formation of the National Constitution. As this was little more than a transcript of prevailing ideas and institutions, it was natural to take the name used in the Declaration of Independence.

And yet it must not be forgotten that there was a name of a different character which was much employed. Congress was called "continental;" the army "continental;" the money "continental,"—a term certainly of unity as well as vastness. But there was still another National designation, accepted at home and abroad. Our country was called "America," and we were called "Americans." Here was a natural, unsought and instinctive name—a growth and not even a creation—implying National unity and predominance, if not exclusive power, on the continent. It was not used occasionally or casually, but constantly; not merely in newspapers, but in official documents. Not an address of Congress; not a military order; not a speech, which does not contain this term, at once so expansive and so unifying. At the opening of the first Continental Congress, Patrick Henry, in another mood from that of a later day, announced the National Unity under this very name. After declaring the boundaries of the several colonies effaced, and the distinctions between Virginians, Pennsylvanians, New Yorkers, and New Englanders as no more, he exclaimed in words of comprehensive patriotism, "I am not a Virginian, but *an American.*" Congress took up the strain and commissioned Washington as commander-in-chief of the armies "for the defence of *American* liberty;" and Washington himself, in his first general order at Cambridge, on assuming his great command, announced that the armies were "for the defence of the liberties of *America;*" and in a letter to Congress just before the battle of Trenton he declared that he had labored "to discourage all kinds of local attachments and distinctions of country, *denominating the whole by the greater name of America.*" Then at the close of the war, in its immortal address, fit supplement to the Declaration of Independence, Congress said: "Let it be remembered that it has ever been the pride and boast of *America* that the rights for which she contended were the rights of Human Nature." And Washington again, in his letter to Congress communicating the National Constitution, says in other words, which, like those of Congress, cannot be too often quoted, that "the *consolidation of the Union* is the greatest interest of *every true American.*" Afterwards in his Farewell Address, which from beginning to end is one persuasive appeal for Nationality, after enjoining upon his fellow-citizens that "*Unity of government* which constitutes them *one people,*" he gives to them a National Name, and this was his legacy: "*The name American, which belongs to you in your National capacity,* must always exalt the just pride of patriotism more than any appellation derived from local discriminations." Thus did Washington put aside all those baneful pretensions under which the country has suffered so much, even to the extent of adopting a National Name, which, like the Union itself, should have a solid coercive power.

It is not impossible that, in the lapse of time, history will vindicate the name adopted by Washington, which may grow as the Republic, until it becomes the natural designation of one country. Our fathers used this term more wisely than they knew; but they acted under Providential guidance. Is it not said of God that he has given names to the stars, "calling them by the greatness of his might?" (*Isaiah*, chap. xl., 26.) Is it not said also that God will make him who overcometh a pillar in the temple and give to him "a new name?" (*Revelation*, chap iii., 12.) So as our stars multiply, and the Nation overcometh its adversaries, persuading all to its declared principles, everywhere on the continent, it will become a pillar in the temple, and the name of the continent itself will be needed to declare alike its unity and its power.

Geographical Unity.

(4.) To these "unities" derived from history and the heart of the people, may be added another where nature is the great teacher; I refer to the geographical position and configuration of our country, if not of the whole continent, marking it for One Nation. Unity is written upon it by the Almighty Hand. In this respect it differs much from Europe, where for generations seas, rivers and mountains kept people apart who had else "Like kindred drops commingled into one." There is no reason why they should not commingle here. Nature in every form is propitious. Facility of intercourse, not less than common advantage, leads to unity; but these are ours. Here are navigable rivers, numerous and famous, being so many highways of travel, and a chain of lakes, each an inland sea. Then there is an unexampled extent of country adapted to railways; and do not forget that with the railway is the telegraph, using the lightning as its messenger, so that the interrogatory of Job is answered, "Canst thou send lightnings that they may go?" The country is one open expanse from the frozen Arctic to the warm waters of the Gulf, and from the Atlantic to the Rocky Mountains, and there science already supplies the means of overcoming this barrier, which in other days would have marked international boundaries. The Pacific Railway will neutralize these mountains and complete the geographical unity of the continent. The slender wire of the telegraph, when once extended, is an indissoluble tie; the railway is an iron band. But these depend upon opportunities which nature supplies, so that nature herself is one of the guardians of our Nationality.

He has studied history poorly, and human nature no better, who imagines that this broad compacted country can be parcelled into different Nationalities. Where will you run the thread of partition? By what river? Along what mountain? On what line of latitude or longitude? Impossible. No line of longitude or latitude, no mountain, no river can become the demarcation. Every state has rights in every other state. The whole country has a title, which it will never renounce, in every part, whether the voluminous Mississippi as it pours to the sea, or that same sea as it chafes upon our coast. As well might we of the East attempt to shut you of the West from the ocean, as you attempt to shut us from the Mississippi. The ocean will always be yours, as it is ours, and the Mississippi will always be ours, as it is yours.

Our country was planned by Providence for a united and homogeneous people. Apparent differences harmonize. Even climate, which passes through all gradations from the North to the South, is so tempered, as to present an easy uniformity from the Atlantic to the Rocky Mountains. Unmeasured supplies of all kinds, mineral and agricultural, are at hand; the richest ores and the most golden crops, with the largest coal-fields of the world below, and the largest corn-fields of the world above. Strabo said of ancient Gaul, that, by its structure, with its vast plains and considerable rivers, it was destined to become the theatre of a great civilization. But the structure of our country is more auspicious. Our plains are vaster and our rivers are more considerable, furnishing a theatre grander than any imagined by the Greek geographer. It is this theatre, thus appointed by nature, which is now open for the good of mankind.

Summary.

Here I stop, to review the field over which we have passed, and to gather its harvest into one sheaf. Beginning with the infancy of the colonies, we have seen how with different names and governments, they were all under *one sovereignty*, with common and interchangeable rights of citizenship, so that no British subject in one colony could be made an alien in any other colony; how even at the beginning longings for a common life began, showing themselves in "loving accord;" how Franklin regarded the colonies as "so many counties;" how the longings increased, until, under the pressure of the mother country, they broke forth in aspirations for "An American Commonwealth;" how they were at last organized in a Congress called from its comprehensive character "Continental;" how, in the exercise of powers derived from the "good people," and in their name, the Continental Congress put forth the Declaration of Independence, by which the sovereignty of the mother country was forever renounced, and we were made "one people," solemnly dedicated to Human Rights, and thus became a Nation; how the undivided sovereignty of all was substituted for the undivided sovereignty of the mother country, and embraced all the states as the other sovereignty had embraced all the colonies; how, according to Franklin, the States were locked together, "so as never to be separated, but by breaking to pieces;" how in an evil hour the Confederation was formed in deference to the denationalizing pretensions of the States; how the longings for national life continued, and found utterance in Congress, in Washington and in patriot compeers; how Jay wished that the States should be like "counties;" how Washington denounced State Sovereignty as "that bantling" and "that monster;" how at last a National Convention assembled, with Washington as President, where it was voted that "a National Government must be established;" how in this spirit, after ample debate, the National Constitution was formed, with its preamble beginning "We the people," with its guaranty of a republican government to all the states, with its investiture of Congress with all needful powers for the maintenance of the government, and with its assertion of supremacy over State Constitutions and laws; how the Constitution was commended by Washington in the name of the Convention as the "consolidation of our Union;" how it was vindicated and opposed as creating a National Government; how on its adoption we again became a Nation; then how our Nationality has been symbolized in the National Flag, the National Motto, and the National Name; and lastly, how nature, in the geographical position and configuration of the country has supplied the means of National Unity, and written her everlasting guaranty. And thus do I now bind the whole together into one conclusion, saying to all, we are a Nation.

Nor is this all. Side by side with the growth of National Unity was a constant dedication to Human Rights, which showed itself, not only in the Declaration of Independence, with its promises and covenants, but in the constant claim of the rights of Magna Charta, the earlier cries of Otis, the assertion, by the first Continental Congress, of the right of the people "to participate in the legislative council," the commission of Washington as Commander-in-chief "in defence of American Liberty," and the first general order of Washington on taking command of his forces, where he rallies them to this cause; also in the later proclamation of Congress, at the close of the Revolution, that the rights contended for had been "the rights of Human Nature," and the farewell general order of Washington, bearing the same date, where the contest is characterized in the same way, so that Human

Rights were the beginning and end of the war, while the Nation, as it grew into being, was quickened by these everlasting principles, and its faith was plighted to their support.

Powers essential to the Nation.

As a Nation, with a place in the family of Nations, we have the powers of a nation, with corresponding responsibilities. Whether we regard these powers as naturally inhering in the Nation, or as conferred upon it by those two title-deeds, the Declaration of Independence and the National Constitution, the conclusion is the same. From nature, and also from its title-deeds, our Nation must have all needful powers, *first*, for the National defence, foremost among which is the power to uphold and defend the National Unity; *secondly*, for the safeguard of the citizen in all his rights of citizenship, foremost among which is Equality the first of rights, so that as all owe equal allegiance, all shall enjoy equal protection; and, *thirdly*, for the support and maintenance of all the promises made by the Nation, especially at its birth, being baptismal vows which cannot be disowned. These three powers are essentially *National.* They belong to our Nation by the very law of its being and the terms of its creation. They cannot be neglected or abandoned. Every person, no matter what his birth, condition or color, who can raise the cry, "I am an American citizen," has a right to require at the hands of the Nation, that it shall do its utmost, by all its central powers, to uphold the National Unity, to protect the citizen in the rights of citizenship, and to perform the original promises of the Nation. Any failure here is apostacy and bankruptcy combined.

It is vain to say that these requirements are not expressly set down in the National Constitution. By a law which existed before this title-deed of our Nation, they belong to the essential conditions of national life. But if not positively nominated in the Constitution, they are there in substance; and this is enough. Every word, from "We the people," to the signature, "George Washington," is instinct with national life, and there is not a single expression taking from the National Government any of its inherent powers. From this "nothing" in the Constitution there can come nothing adverse to these powers. But there has always been in the Constitution a positive injunction on the Nation to guaranty "a republican form of government" to all the States; and who can doubt that, in the execution of this guaranty, the Nation may exercise all these powers, and provide especially for the protection of the citizen in all the rights of citizenship? There are also recent amendments of the Constitution abolishing slavery, and expressly securing the "privileges and immunities of citizens" against the pretensions of States. Then there is the Declaration of Independence itself, which is the earlier title-deed. By that sacred instrument we were declared to be "one people," with Liberty and Equality for all, and then, fixing forever the rights of citizenship, it was announced that all just government was derived only from "the consent of the governed." Come weal or woe, that great Declaration must stand forever. Other things may fail, but this cannot fail. It is immortal as the Nation itself. It is a part of the Nation, and is that part most worthy of immortality. By it the Constitution must be interpreted, or rather the two together are our Constitution—as Magna Charta and the Bill of Rights together are the British Constitution. By the Declaration our Nation was born and its vital principles were announced. By the Constitution the Nation was born again and supplied with the machinery of government. The two together are our National Scriptures, each being a Testament.

Adverse Pretension of State Rights.

Against this conclusion there has been from the beginning one perpetual pretension in the name of State Rights. The same spirit, which has been so hostile to National Unity in other countries; which made each feudal chief a petty sovereign; which for a long time convulsed France; which for centuries divided Italy, and which unhappily still divides Germany, has appeared among us. Assuming that communities, which were never "sovereign" while colonies, and which became independent only by the National power, had in some way, by some sudden hocus-pocus, leaped into local sovereignty, and forgetting also that two sovereignties cannot co-exist in the same place, as according to the early dramatist,

> "Two kings in England cannot reign at once,"

the States insisted upon sovereign powers justly belonging to the Nation. Long ago the Duel began. The partisans of State Rights, plausibly professing to *decentralize* the government, have done everything possible to *denationalize* it. In the name of self-government they have organized local lordships hostile to Human Rights. In the name of the States, they have sacrificed the Nation.

This pretension which has constantly shown itself, has broken out on three principal occasions. The first was in the effort of nullification, which occurred in 1833, where, under the lead of Mr. Calhoun, South Carolina attempted to nullify the revenue acts of Congress, or, in other words, to declare them void within her limits. After encountering the matchless argument of Daniel Webster, enforced by his best eloquence, nullification was blasted by the thunder-bolt of Andrew Jackson, who, in his Proclamation as President thus exposed it, even in the form of secession, which it assumed at a later day: "Each State, having expressly parted with so many powers as to constitute jointly with other States a *single Nation*, cannot after that period possess any right to secede, because such secession does not break a league, but destroys the Unity of a Nation." The pretension next showed itself in the Rebellion. And now that the Rebellion has been crushed, it re-appears in still another form, by insisting that each State at its own will may disregard the universal rights of the citizen, and apply a discrimination according to its own local prejudices; thus within its borders nullifying the primal truths of the Declaration of Independence. Here again do State Rights, in their anarchical egotism, interfere with the National Unity.

The National Supremacy consistent with Local Self-Government.

Local self-government, whether in the town, county or state, is of incalculable advantage, supplying the opportunities of political education, and also a local administration adapted precisely to local wants. On this account the system has been admired by travellers from abroad, who have found in our "town-meetings" the nurseries of the Republic, and have delighted in local exemption from central supervisorship. DeTocqueville, who journeyed here, has recorded his authoritative praise, and Laboulaye, who has visited us only in his remarkable studies, unites with De Toqueville. Against that exacting centralization, absorbing everything to itself, of which Paris is the example, I oppose the American system of self government, which leaves the people to themselves, subject only to the paramount conditions of national life. But these conditions cannot be sacrificed. No local claim of self-government can for a moment interfere with the supremacy of the Nation, in the maintenance of Human Rights.

According to the wisdom of Plutarch, we must shun those pestilent persons who would "carry trifles to the highest magistrate," and, in the same spirit, we must reject that pestilent supervisorship which asserts a regulating power over local affairs, and thus becomes a giant intermeddler. Let these be decided at home in the states, counties and towns to which they belong. Such is the genius of our institutions. This is the precious principle of self-government which is at once educator and agency. In the former character, it is an omnipresent schoolmaster; in the latter, it is a suit of "chain-armor," which, from its flexibility, is adapted to the body of the Nation, so that all the limbs are free. Each locality has its own way in all matters peculiar to itself. But the rights of all must be placed under the protection of all; nor can there be any difference in different parts of the country. Here the rule must be uniform, and it must be sustained by the central power radiating to every part of the various empire. This is according to the divine Cosmos, which in all its spaces is pervaded by one universal law; it is the rule of Almighty beneficence, which, while leaving human beings to the activities of daily life and the consciousness of free will, subjects all to the same commanding principles. Such centralization is the highest civilization, for it approaches the nearest to the Heavenly example. Call it imperialism, if you please; it is simply the imperialism of the Declaration of Independence, with all its promises fulfilled. It is rendering unto Cæsar the things that are Cæsar's. Already by central power Slavery has been abolished. Already by central power all have been assured in the Equality of *civil* rights.

> ———— "Two truths are told
> As happy prologues to the swelling act
> Of the imperial theme."

It remains now that by central power all should be assured in the Equality of *political* rights. This does not involve necessarily what is sometimes called the "regulation" of the suffrage by the National Government, although this would be best. It simply requires the abolition of any discrimination among citizens, inconsistent with Equal Rights. If not by act of Congress, let it be by a new amendment of the Constitution; but it must be at once. Until this is done, we leave undone what ought to be done, and, in our pitiable failure to perform a National duty, justify the saying, that "there is no health in us." The preposterous pretension, that color, whether of the hair or of the skin, or that any other unchangeable circumstance of natural condition may be made the "qualification" of a voter, cannot be tolerated. It is shocking to the moral sense and degrading to the understanding.

As in the Nation there can be but one Sovereignty, so there can be but one citizenship. The unity of Sovereignty finds its counterpart and complement in the unity of citizenship, and the two together are the tokens of a united people. Thus are the essential conditions of national life all resolved into three; *One Sovereignty*, *One Citizenship*, *One People.*

Conclusion.

I conclude as I began. The late Rebellion against the Nation was in the name of State Rights; therefore State Rights in their denationalizing pretensions must be overthrown. It proceeded from hostility to the sacred principles of the Declaration of Independence; therefore, these sacred principles must be vindicated in spirit and in letter, so that hereafter they shall be a supreme law, co-equal with the Constitution, in whose illumination the Constitution must be read, and they shall supply the final definition of a Republic for our guidance at home and for an example to mankind.

In this great change we follow nature and obey her mandate. By an irresistible law, water everywhere seeks its level and finds it; and so, by a law as irresistible, man seeks the level of every other man in rights, and will find it. Human passions and human institutions are unavailing to arrest it,—as nature is stronger than man, and the Creator is mightier than the creature. The recognition of this law is essential to the national cause, for so you will work with nature rather than against it, and at the same time in harmony with the Declaration of Independence. Here I borrow a word from Locke, who, in his Essay on the Human Understanding says that, in dealing with propositions, we must always find on what they "bottom." Now, in dealing with the Rebellion, we find that though in the name of State Rights, it "bottomed" on opposition to the law of nature and an open denial of the self-evident truths declared by our Fathers, especially of that central truth of all, which Abraham Lincoln, at Gettysburg, in the most touching speech of all history thus announces: "Fourscore and seven years ago our fathers brought forth on this continent a New Nation, conceived in Liberty, and dedicated to the proposition that *all men are created equal.*" Slavery was "bottomed" on the direct opposite; and so was the Rebellion, from beginning to end. Therefore you must encounter this denial. You do not extinguish Slavery; you do not trample out the Rebellion, until the vital truth declared by our Fathers is established and nature in her law is obeyed. To complete the good work this must be done. Liberty has been won; Equality must be won also. In England, there is Liberty without Equality; in France, Equality without Liberty. The two together must be ours. This final victory will be the greatest of the war; it will be the consummation of all other victories. Here must we plant the National standard. To this championship I now summon you. Go forth, victors in so many fields, and gather now the highest palm of all. The victory of ideas is grander far than any victory of blood. What battle ever did so much for Humanity as the sermon on Mars Hill? What battle ever did so much as the Declaration of Independence? But sermon and Declaration re one, and it is your glorious part to assure the National Unity n this adamantine base.

All hail to the Republic, redeemed and regenerated, one and ıdivisible. Nullification and secession are already like the extinct monsters of a former geological period—to be seen only in the museum of history. With their extinction must disappear that captious, litigious and disturbing spirit engendered by State Rights. The whole face of the country will be transformed. There will be concord for discord; smiles for frowns. There will be a new consciousness of national life with a corresponding glow. The soul will dilate with the assured Unity of the Republic, and all will feel the glory of its citizenship. Since that of Rome nothing has been so commanding. Local jealousies and geographical distinctions will be lost in the attractions of a common country. Then, indeed, there will be no North, no South, no East, no West; but there will be One Nation. No single point of the compass, but the whole horizon will receive our regard. Not the southern cross flaming with beauty; not even the north star, so long the guide of the mariner and the refuge to the flying bondman, but the whole star-spread firmament will be our worship and delight.

As the Nation stands confessed in undivided sovereignty, the states will not cease to perform their appropriate functions. Interlaced, interlocked and harmonized, they will be congenial parts of the mighty whole, while Liberty and Equality will be the recognized birthright of all, and no local pretension can interfere against the universal law. There will be a sphere alike for the States and Nation. Local self-government, which is the pride of our institutions, will be reconciled with the National supremacy in the maintenance of Human Rights, and the two together will be the elemental principles of the Republic. The states will exercise a minute jurisdiction required for the convenience of all; the Nation will exercise that other paramount jurisdiction required for the protection of all. The reconciliation—God bless the word!—thus begun will embrace the people, who, forgetting past differences, will feel more than ever that they are one, and it will invigorate the still growing Republic, whose original root was little more than an acorn, so that it will find new strength to resist the shock of tempest or time, while it overarches the continent with its generous shade. Such at least is the aspiration in which all may unite.

"Firm like the oak, may our blest Nation rise,
No less distinguished for its strength than size;
The unequal branches emulous unite
To shield and grace the trunk's majestic height;
Through long succeeding years and centuries live,
No vigor losing from the aid they give."

www.ingramcontent.com/pod-product-compliance
Lightning Source LLC
LaVergne TN
LVHW011122110826
845150LV00008B/2221

* 9 7 8 1 4 1 8 1 9 5 1 5 1 *